St. Lucia Trave

2025–2026

Discover The Ultimate Vacation Planner with Itineraries, Local Tips, Hiding Gems, and Things to Do on the Caribbean's Most Beautiful Island

Luis F. Brown

Disclaimer

This travel guide is designed to help you discover the natural beauty, vibrant culture, and unforgettable experiences that St. Lucia has to offer. From the iconic Pitons and tropical beaches to charming fishing villages and lively street festivals, this book provides practical tips, local insights, and helpful suggestions to make your journey across the island meaningful and enjoyable.

Please note: Every effort has been made to ensure the accuracy of the information in this edition. However, travel-related details—such as business hours, ferry schedules, entry requirements, prices, and event dates—can change from time to time. Travelers are encouraged to double-check key information through official websites, trusted travel platforms, or local tourism offices before making final plans.

This guide is meant to be a friendly companion to enhance your adventure—not a final authority on all things St. Lucia. We invite you to use it with an open heart, a flexible spirit, and a sense of curiosity.

St. Lucia is not just a destination—it's an experience that stays with you.

Table Of Contents

Introduction

I have traveled to different islands before, but this year, in 2025, I finally visited St. Lucia for the first time—and it was more than I ever dreamed. I had heard people talk about how beautiful the island was, but being there myself was something truly special. From the moment I arrived, I knew this trip would be different. It felt like the island was calling me, welcoming me with open arms.

As soon as I stepped off the plane, I was met with warm sunshine and the smell of the ocean. The sky was blue, the air was fresh, and the sound of reggae music playing in the background made me smile. A local driver named Elijah picked me up, and he was one of the friendliest people I've ever met. On the way to my hotel, he told me stories about the island and pointed out spots I should visit. His love for

St. Lucia made me even more excited to explore.

I stayed near the town of Soufrière, surrounded by green hills and the famous Pitons—two tall mountains that rise straight out of the sea. Seeing them with my own eyes for the first time gave me chills. I couldn't stop staring. Every morning, I'd sit on my balcony with a cup of coffee, watching the sunrise behind those mountains. It felt peaceful and perfect.

One of the best days of my trip was hiking up Gros Piton. It was a bit of a challenge, but I had a local guide named Marie who made the experience fun and inspiring. She told me about the island's history and how important nature is to the people here. When we got to the top, the view took my breath away. I could see the ocean stretching far into the distance. I just stood there in silence, feeling thankful.

I also visited the Sulphur Springs, where I covered myself in warm volcanic mud. They say it's good for your skin, but what I loved most was the laughter and joy shared with others there. After the mud bath, we rinsed off under a cool waterfall. That moment felt like a scene from a movie.

One night, I went to the Gros Islet Friday Night Street Party. The streets were full of music, dancing, and the smell of delicious food. I tried grilled fish, local juice, and even learned a few dance moves from the locals. Everyone was kind and happy. It was one of those nights where time didn't matter—I was just enjoying life.

St. Lucia touched my heart. It's more than just a place to visit. It's a place to feel, to breathe, and to reconnect with what really matters. If you're thinking about visiting, don't wait. Let this island show you its magic. I came as a visitor, but I left feeling like part of the island.

Chapter 1: Welcome to St. Lucia

A Brief History of St. Lucia

St. Lucia's story is one of strength, culture, and beauty. Long before tourists arrived, the island was home to the **Arawaks** and later the **Caribs**, two groups of Indigenous people who lived off the land and sea. They fished in the clear waters and farmed in the rich volcanic soil. They called the island "**Iouanalao**," meaning "Land of the Iguanas."

In the 1600s, European powers arrived. Both **the French and the British** wanted control of the island. For over 150 years, they fought back and forth—St. Lucia changed hands between them **14 times**! This is why you'll find both French and English influences here today—in names, food, and culture.

The British finally took control in the early 1800s. They brought enslaved Africans to work on sugar plantations. Even after slavery ended in 1834, life was not easy, but the people of St. Lucia were proud and resilient. Over time, they built strong communities rooted in family, faith, and tradition.

St. Lucia gained full independence from Britain on **February 22, 1979**, but it remains a part of the **Commonwealth of Nations**. Today, it's a peaceful and vibrant nation, where people still celebrate their African, French, and British roots with pride.

When you visit, you'll see this history everywhere—from the colonial buildings in Castries to the French-inspired names of towns like Soufrière and Choiseul. But most of all, you'll feel it in the spirit of the people—warm, proud, and always ready to share their stories.

What's New for 2025–2026

St. Lucia continues to grow as a favorite travel destination, and in 2025–2026, there are exciting new things to see and do.

Several new eco-friendly resorts have opened across the island, especially near **Vieux Fort** and **Marigot Bay**. These resorts are designed with nature in mind—built using local materials, powered by solar energy, and committed to protecting the island's environment.

There's also a focus on **community tourism** in 2025. Travelers can now book local tours led by St. Lucians themselves—fishermen, farmers, artists, and even chefs. These tours offer real insight into daily life, allowing you to connect with people and support the local economy directly.

New hiking trails have been added near the **Edmund Forest Reserve**, perfect for nature lovers. These well-marked paths offer quiet escapes, where you can spot rare birds and take in the tropical beauty of St. Lucia's untouched rainforest.

In Castries, the **Central Market** has received a major upgrade. You'll find more local vendors, food stalls, and handmade crafts than ever before. It's the perfect place to taste Creole snacks or pick up a handwoven basket made right before your eyes.

Technology is also improving the travel experience. The **Hewanorra International Airport** is being expanded with faster customs, more shopping, and better service for arriving visitors. Many tour companies now offer easy online bookings, and digital travel apps help visitors navigate the island without hassle.

Whether you're a returning traveler or it's your first time, St. Lucia in 2025–2026 is fresh, exciting, and full of local charm.

Embracing St. Lucian Culture & Language

St. Lucian culture is colorful, joyful, and deeply rooted in tradition. When you visit, you won't just see a beautiful island—you'll meet people with a rich heritage and a big heart.

One of the best ways to understand the culture is through **music**. Whether it's the sound of **calypso, soca, or steel pan**, music fills the air, especially during festivals like **Carnival** or **Jounen Kwéyòl (Creole Day)**. You'll see people dancing, wearing colorful clothes, and celebrating together like family.

Food is another window into St. Lucian life. Try local dishes like **green fig and saltfish** (the national dish), **bouyon** (a hearty stew), and fresh grilled fish. Meals are often enjoyed with family and friends, and sharing food is a big part of hospitality here.

Language plays a special role too. English is the official language, but many people speak **Kwéyòl** (St. Lucian Creole), a mix of French, African, and Caribbean words. You might hear someone say "**Bonjour**" (Good morning) or "**Sa ka fèt?**" (What's happening?). Don't be shy—locals love it when visitors try to speak a little Creole!

Faith is also important. Most people are Christian, and churches are central to village life. You might hear gospel music on a Sunday morning or see beautifully dressed families heading to service.

St. Lucians are proud of their identity. They are warm, respectful, and happy to share their island with you. When you support local artists, buy handmade crafts, or take a village tour, you're not just learning—you're helping preserve a unique way of life.

Take time to slow down, greet people with a smile, and soak in the rhythm of the island. Culture in St. Lucia isn't something you just watch—it's something you feel. And once you feel it, you'll never forget it.

Chapter 2: Getting Ready

When to Go: Seasons, Festivals & Weather

St. Lucia is beautiful all year round, but the best time to visit depends on what kind of experience you want.

Weather-wise, the island has two main seasons: the **dry season** and the **wet season**. The dry season runs from **December to May**. This is the most popular time for tourists. The days are sunny and warm, with lower humidity and very little rain. If you're planning to hike the Pitons or enjoy beach days without worrying about showers, this is a great time to visit. However, since it’s peak season, flights and hotels tend to be more expensive.

The **wet season**, from **June to November**, brings more rain and the chance of tropical storms. But don't worry—it rarely rains all day. Most times, it rains in short bursts and then clears up. This is also the **off-season**, so prices are lower, and there are fewer crowds. It's a great time for budget travelers or those who enjoy a more peaceful vibe.

St. Lucia also comes alive with **festivals and cultural events** throughout the year. One of the biggest is the **Saint Lucia Jazz & Arts Festival**, held in **May**. This world-famous event features live music, dancing, art, and food. It's a fantastic way to experience the island's culture.

In **July**, the island celebrates **Carnival**, a colorful event filled with parades, costumes, street parties, and music. If you enjoy lively celebrations, this is a perfect time to visit.

For a quieter but meaningful experience, visit during **Creole Heritage Month** in **October**, when locals celebrate their language, food, and traditions.

In summary, if you want the best weather, visit between **December and May**. If you want better deals and fewer tourists, go between **June and November**. No matter when you visit, there's always something special happening on the island.

Budget Breakdown & Average Costs

Planning your travel budget for St. Lucia can help you make the most of your trip without surprises. Here's a simple guide to what things typically cost in 2025.

Flights: Airfare depends on where you're coming from. From the U.S. or Canada, round-trip flights usually range from **$400 to $900** depending on the season. Booking early or flying mid-week can save you money.

Accommodation: St. Lucia offers everything from budget guesthouses to luxury resorts. On average:

- Budget stay: **$50–$100/night**
- Mid-range hotel: **$120–$250/night**
- High-end resorts: **$300–$1000+/night**

Food & Drinks: If you eat at local spots or food stands, you can have a delicious meal for about **$10–$15**. A nice dinner at a restaurant can cost **$25–$50 per person**, especially with drinks. Groceries are available if you're staying somewhere with a kitchen.

Transportation: Taxis are common but can be pricey. A short ride can cost **$20–$40**. Renting a car costs around **$60–$90 per day**. You can also use local minibuses, which are cheap (around **$2 per ride**) but don't always run on a set schedule.

Attractions & Tours:

- Sulphur Springs or mud baths: **$10–$15**
- Piton hike with guide: **$50–$100**
- Boat tours or snorkeling trips: **$60–$120**

Daily Budget Estimate:

- Budget traveler: **$100/day**
- Mid-range: **$150–$250/day**

- Luxury: **$300–$600/day**

To save money, travel in the off-season, book activities ahead, and enjoy local food. Many of the island's natural wonders—like beaches, hikes, and scenic drives—are free or very affordable.

Packing List Essentials

Packing smartly for St. Lucia will help you feel comfortable and ready for anything, from beach days to rainforest hikes. Here's what you should bring:

Clothing:

- Light, breathable clothes like T-shirts, shorts, sundresses

- Swimsuits (bring 2–3 so you always have a dry one)
- Flip-flops or sandals for the beach
- Comfortable walking shoes or sneakers
- Light jacket or sweater for cool nights or air-conditioned places
- Rain poncho or small umbrella (especially if visiting during the wet season)

Outdoor & Adventure Gear:

- Reusable water bottle
- Daypack or small backpack for tours and hikes

- Reef-safe sunscreen (very important to protect the marine life)
- Sunglasses and a wide-brim hat for sun protection
- Bug spray or mosquito repellent
- Snorkel gear if you prefer using your own

Health & Safety:

- Basic first-aid kit (band-aids, pain relievers, etc.)
- Any medications you take regularly

- Hand sanitizer and antibacterial wipes
- Travel insurance details

Tech & Travel Documents:

- Phone and charger
- Portable power bank
- Waterproof pouch for your phone and valuables
- Passport (valid for at least 6 months)
- Printouts or digital copies of hotel reservations and tour bookings
- Driver's license if you plan to rent a car

Optional but Helpful:

- Travel guidebook or map
- Small flashlight or headlamp (useful if exploring less developed areas)
- Lightweight towel or beach mat
- Snacks for excursions or travel days

Remember, the island is casual, so there's no need to overpack. Bring what you need to stay cool, comfortable, and safe—and leave room for souvenirs!

Chapter 3: Sample Itineraries

Romantic 5-Day Honeymoon Highlights

St. Lucia is one of the most romantic places in the Caribbean. With its beautiful beaches, mountain views, and cozy resorts, it's perfect for couples who want to relax and enjoy each other. This 5-day honeymoon plan will help you enjoy the best of love and nature.

Day 1: Arrival and Sunset Welcome

Arrive in St. Lucia and check into a romantic hotel in Soufrière or near the Pitons. Many couples stay at places like Jade Mountain, Ladera, or Sugar Beach. Take it slow. Enjoy a welcome drink, relax by the pool, and end your day with a candlelight dinner while watching the sunset over the Caribbean Sea.

Day 2: Spa & Sulphur Springs Experience

Start your day with a couple's spa treatment or massage. Then head to the Sulphur Springs for a mud bath—locals say it's good for the skin. After rinsing off at a waterfall, have lunch in town and spend the evening enjoying drinks at your resort.

Day 3: Piton Cruise & Beach Picnic

Take a private catamaran cruise around the island. Stop to snorkel or swim at Anse Chastanet or Sugar Beach. Arrange for a picnic on the sand with local dishes like grilled fish and fried plantains. End the day watching the stars from your balcony.

Day 4: Explore Local Culture

Visit the colorful Castries Market to shop for handmade gifts and spices. Then explore Pigeon

Island for history, sea views, and an easy hike. Enjoy lunch at a waterfront café and spend your afternoon relaxing at Reduit Beach.

Day 5: Final Breakfast & Departure

On your last morning, enjoy a slow breakfast with a view. Take a short walk along the beach before checking out. Your honeymoon may be ending, but the memories will stay with you forever.

Adventure 7-Day Island Explorer

For travelers who love excitement and nature, St. Lucia is a paradise. This 7-day itinerary includes hiking, water sports, and exploring local spots while still having time to relax.

Day 1: Arrival and Settle In

Arrive and check into a guesthouse or adventure-friendly lodge. Spend the day exploring nearby beaches or going for a walk around your hotel. Prepare for an active week ahead!

Day 2: Gros Piton Hike

Wake up early for the famous Gros Piton hike. It takes about 4–5 hours round trip. The view from the top is stunning! After the hike, enjoy a local meal and spend the rest of the day resting or swimming.

Day 3: Water Adventure Day

Take a full-day snorkeling or diving tour to places like Anse Cochon or the marine reserve near Anse Chastanet. If you prefer kayaking or paddleboarding, that's also a fun way to explore the coast.

Day 4: Ziplining & Rainforest Hike

Head to the Treetop Adventure Park for ziplining through the rainforest. Then explore one of the island's nature trails, like Edmund

Forest Reserve, where you can see birds, waterfalls, and rare plants.

Day 5: Road Trip to East Coast

Rent a car or take a tour to the island's quieter side. Visit places like Dennery and Grande Anse, known for their cliffs and natural views. Stop at a beach for lunch and enjoy the peaceful vibe away from the crowds.

Day 6: Culture and History

Spend your day visiting Pigeon Island National Park, which has old fort ruins, lovely beaches, and beautiful views. You can also check out local museums or art galleries. Enjoy some island music in the evening.

Day 7: Relax & Depart

Take your final morning slow. Visit a beach one last time or shop for souvenirs. Reflect on your amazing week before heading to the airport.

Budget-Friendly 4-Day Weekend Escape

If you only have a few days and want to enjoy St. Lucia without spending too much, this plan helps you enjoy the island on a budget—without missing out on fun.

Day 1: Arrival & Beach Chill

Fly in and check into an affordable guesthouse or Airbnb near Rodney Bay or Gros Islet. After settling in, head to Reduit Beach. It's free, beautiful, and has a fun vibe. Enjoy some local food at a beachside grill and watch the sunset.

Day 2: Pigeon Island & Local Food

Walk or take a short ride to Pigeon Island National Park. The entrance fee is low, and you can hike, relax by the water, or explore the old ruins. Bring your own lunch or buy something from a local vendor. In the evening, head to Gros Islet for the famous Friday Night Street Party—great food, music, and fun with locals!

Day 3: Soufrière Day Trip

Take a budget tour or shared minibus to Soufrière. Visit the Sulphur Springs and take a mud bath, then rinse off at the nearby waterfall. You can pack your own snacks or grab lunch from a local café. End your trip with a beach visit before heading back.

Day 4: Markets & Departure

Spend your last morning walking around the Castries Market. It's free to browse, and you can pick up handmade souvenirs, spices, or snacks. Enjoy a relaxed breakfast, then head to the airport feeling refreshed and happy.

Chapter 4: North Coast & Castries

Castries Markets & Waterfront Promenade

Castries, the capital city of St. Lucia, is the perfect place to begin your adventure. It's a busy, colorful place where island life feels alive and full of energy. One of the best things to do in Castries is visit the local markets, especially the **Castries Central Market**. It's a big, open-air space where friendly vendors sell everything from fresh fruits and spices to handmade crafts and souvenirs.

As you walk through the market, you'll smell the sweet scent of ripe mangoes, spices like cinnamon and nutmeg, and local dishes being cooked nearby. You'll hear local music playing and people chatting and laughing. It’s a great place to try something new—maybe a local coconut cake or a cold bottle of Piton beer. And if you're looking for souvenirs, this is where you’ll find handmade baskets, jewelry, and art made by local artisans.

Just a few steps away is the **Waterfront Promenade**, which gives you a peaceful view of the harbor. Watch the cruise ships come in, or sit on a bench with a snack and enjoy the sea breeze. The promenade is also lined with local shops and cafes. It's the perfect spot to take a break, enjoy a drink, and do a bit of people-watching.

If you’re there on a day when cruise ships dock, Castries gets lively. Tourists and locals mix, and the streets fill with music, movement, and color. Even if crowds aren’t your thing, it's worth seeing at least once.

Castries may be small, but it has a big heart. The markets and waterfront area show a side of the island that's real, friendly, and full of charm. Take your time here, chat with the locals, try the street food, and soak in the Caribbean spirit that fills every corner of this lovely city.

Pigeon Island National Park

Pigeon Island National Park is one of the most beautiful and historic places in St. Lucia. Even though it's no longer a true island (it was connected to the mainland by a causeway), it still feels like its own little world. Whether you love nature, history, or just want a peaceful spot to relax, Pigeon Island has something for you.

Start by taking a walk through the park's trails. You'll see old stone ruins, green hills, and wide ocean views. The park is home to the remains of **Fort Rodney**, a British military base used in the 1700s. Climbing up to the top of the fort is a must. The view from there is stunning—you can see across to Martinique on a clear day, and you'll definitely want to take some photos.

If you're not into hiking, that's okay too. The lower parts of the park have picnic areas, shaded benches, and quiet beaches where you can swim or just lay in the sun. The water is calm and clear, perfect for snorkeling or a relaxing float. There's even a small beach bar nearby where you can grab a drink or a bite to eat.

Keep your eyes open for wildlife too! You might see small birds, lizards, and maybe even a mongoose. Everything feels peaceful here. You can walk slowly, breathe in the fresh air, and take a break from busy life.

Entry to the park costs a small fee, but it's worth every penny. Bring water, comfortable shoes, and your camera. And don't forget sunscreen—it can get very sunny out there.

Pigeon Island is a great mix of nature and history. It's a place where you can feel the past and enjoy the present at the same time. Whether you're traveling solo, as a couple, or with family, this is one stop you'll never forget on your visit to St. Lucia.

Gros Islet Friday Night Street Party

If you want to feel the true spirit of St. Lucia, don't miss the **Gros Islet Friday Night Street Party**. It happens every Friday evening in the fishing village of Gros Islet, just north of Castries. What starts as a quiet town during the day turns into a lively, colorful celebration once the sun goes down.

The streets fill with music—mostly reggae, soca, and dancehall—and the smell of grilled fish, jerk chicken, and barbecue fills the air. Locals set up stalls and small grills, cooking right on the street. You'll find everything from spicy seafood to sweet local treats. Try the grilled lobster or fish with Creole sauce—it's full of flavor and made with love.

It's not just about food. People come here to dance, laugh, and enjoy life together. There's no need to be shy—everyone is welcome. Locals and tourists dance in the streets, and there's usually a DJ or live band playing on loudspeakers. Even if you don't dance, the energy is fun and contagious.

You can also find small shops selling handmade crafts, local rum, and souvenirs. It's a great time to support local vendors and take home something special. The prices are usually better than in the tourist shops, and you get to meet the people who made the items.

The best part of the Gros Islet Street Party is how real it feels. It's not a show put on for tourists—it's something the community truly enjoys. Everyone's invited, and the vibe is welcoming and friendly. You can come alone and leave with new friends.

If you're visiting St. Lucia, try to plan your stay around Friday night so you can experience this event. Bring cash, wear comfortable clothes, and just go with the flow. This isn't a fancy event—it's about joy, music, and community.

By the end of the night, with a full stomach and a happy heart, you'll understand why so many people say this is the best night out on the island. It's a memory you'll carry home with you, long after your trip is over.

Chapter 5: Soufrière & The Pitons

Hiking Gros and Petit Pitons

The Pitons are the most famous landmarks in St. Lucia—and for good reason. These two striking volcanic mountains, Gros Piton and Petit Piton, rise dramatically from the sea near the town of Soufrière. They are not only stunning to look at, but also offer exciting hiking experiences for visitors.

Gros Piton is the larger of the two, standing at about 2,618 feet. This is the mountain most travelers choose to hike. It takes around 4 to 5 hours to complete the round trip, and while it's not easy, it's totally worth it. The trail is steep in parts, especially the second half, but it's well-marked and guided. Hiring a local guide is required—and it's a good thing! Your guide will keep you safe, share stories, and point out plants, birds, and even hidden views you might miss on your own.

At the top, you'll be rewarded with breathtaking views of the island and the Caribbean Sea. The sense of achievement and beauty at that moment is something you'll never forget.

Petit Piton, although smaller at around 2,438 feet, is much steeper and more challenging. It’s not recommended for beginners or casual hikers. Climbing Petit Piton involves using ropes and climbing steep rock faces. Only experienced hikers should attempt this, and always with a certified guide.

Whether you take on Gros Piton or just admire the Pitons from a distance, they are truly a highlight of St. Lucia. Don’t forget your water, sturdy shoes, and camera. And most importantly, take your time—this is not just a hike, it's an unforgettable adventure.

Sulphur Springs Volcano & Mud Baths

Located just outside Soufrière, Sulphur Springs is one of St. Lucia's most unique and fascinating attractions. It's known as the "Caribbean's only drive-in volcano," because you can actually drive right into the crater. Don't worry—though the volcano is still active, it's safe to visit.

As you arrive, the smell of sulfur (a bit like boiled eggs) lets you know you're in volcanic territory. Steam rises from the bubbling hot pools, and your guide will explain how the area was formed. The history here is incredible. Long ago, volcanic activity shaped much of the island, and the Sulphur Springs are a living reminder of nature's power.

But the real fun comes with the **mud baths**. After the short tour, visitors are invited to jump into warm mineral-rich pools and slather their bodies with gray volcanic mud. The mud is said to have healing powers—good for the skin, joints, and even sunburn. Whether you believe in its benefits or not, the experience is pure joy. People laugh, paint designs on each other with the mud, and take photos with gray faces and big smiles.

After covering yourself with mud, you rinse off in hot spring water that flows naturally from the earth. Your skin will feel soft and refreshed afterward.

It's a fun, relaxing, and memorable stop that's great for couples, families, or solo travelers. Make sure to bring a dark swimsuit (the mud can stain), a towel, and a sense of adventure. The Sulphur Springs is more than a tourist spot—it's a moment of connection with the earth, and a chance to enjoy nature in a playful way.

Diamond Botanical Gardens & Toraille Waterfall

Just a short drive from central Soufrière, the **Diamond Botanical Gardens** offer a peaceful escape into the heart of St. Lucia's natural beauty. This six-acre garden is one of the oldest in the Caribbean and has been delighting visitors for years with its mix of tropical plants, colorful flowers, and historic charm.

As you stroll along the shaded paths, you'll see tall bamboo, bright hibiscus, orchids, and flowering trees in every direction. It's a quiet place, perfect for relaxing, taking photos, or just enjoying the calm. There's also a small stream that flows through the gardens, adding to the peaceful atmosphere.

One of the main highlights is the **Diamond Waterfall**, which is unlike any other in the Caribbean. The water flows down a rock face colored by minerals like sulfur, copper, and iron, which give it beautiful shades of green, yellow, and orange. It's a stunning sight, especially after rain when the water flows faster. Though you can't swim in the waterfall, it makes a perfect backdrop for pictures.

Nearby, there are mineral baths that date back to the 18th century, originally built for French soldiers. Today, you can enjoy a warm soak in the same natural waters that flow from the volcano. It's a relaxing experience, especially after a long day of exploring.

A visit to the Diamond Botanical Gardens and Waterfall is great for travelers of all ages. It's not a long hike, and the paths are easy to walk. You can take your time, enjoy the beauty of the plants and flowers, and maybe even spot a hummingbird or two.

If you're visiting Soufrière, don't miss this peaceful little gem. It's a reminder of just how lush and colorful St. Lucia really is.

Chapter 6: East Coast & Atlantic Beaches

Grande Anse & Reduit Beach

St. Lucia's east coast is less crowded than the west, but it's full of hidden treasures—like Grande Anse and Reduit Beach. These two beaches offer very different experiences, making them perfect stops for all kinds of travelers.

Grande Anse is one of the most peaceful beaches on the island. You won't find crowds here—just the sound of waves, sea birds, and coconut trees swaying in the wind. It's not a swimming beach because the waves are strong, but it's perfect for walking, relaxing, or even spotting sea turtles. In fact, this beach is a nesting ground for leatherback turtles, especially between March and August. If you're lucky, you might witness baby turtles making their way to the ocean—it's magical.

The journey to Grande Anse can be a little bumpy, as the road is unpaved in some areas. But if you enjoy exploring untouched nature and taking photos of wild, beautiful landscapes, this is a must-visit. Bring water, snacks, and your camera.

Reduit Beach, on the other hand, is lively and popular—especially for families and couples. Located in Rodney Bay, this beach is known for its golden sand and calm, swimmable waters. There are plenty of restaurants, bars, and water sports available here. You can rent a jet ski, try paddleboarding, or just float in the clear water.

Reduit is also close to shopping and nightlife, so you can easily spend a full day here. Whether you want a quiet moment under a palm tree or an exciting ride on a banana boat, Reduit has something for you.

Together, Grande Anse and Reduit Beach show the two sides of St. Lucia's east coast—untouched natural beauty and fun beach life. Both are worth a visit during your stay.

Anse La Raye & Canaries Bay

Anse La Raye and Canaries Bay are two charming fishing villages along St. Lucia's coastline that offer a real taste of local life.

They are quiet, colorful, and full of warm, welcoming people.

Anse La Raye is a small village with a big heart. Its name means “Bay of Rays,” and it was once home to large numbers of stingrays. Today, it’s known for its Friday night fish fry, where locals and visitors come together to enjoy grilled seafood, music, and dancing right by the sea. Even during the week, Anse La Raye has a peaceful vibe. You can stroll through the village, talk with friendly residents, and watch the fishermen bring in their daily catch.

There are also beautiful waterfalls nearby—like Anse La Raye Falls—that make great stops if you love nature and adventure. The hike is short and enjoyable, and the cool water at the end is refreshing.

Canaries Bay, just a short drive from Anse La Raye, is one of the least touristy spots on the island. This makes it feel authentic and special. The beach is small but clean and quiet, perfect for a picnic or a relaxing afternoon. The village itself is built along the hill, and you can see colorful houses stacked like stairs above the sea.

Canaries is a great place to try fresh bread from a local bakery or chat with an elder who may share stories of the past. It's simple, calm, and feels like a step back in time—in the best way.

These two villages are ideal for travelers who want to see the real St. Lucia, beyond the resorts. Spend a day visiting both—you won't regret it.

Dennery's Fishing Villages & Sunday Fish Fry

Dennery is one of the most vibrant places on the east coast of St. Lucia. Known for its strong fishing traditions, music, and colorful houses, this area offers visitors an unforgettable cultural experience—especially on Sunday nights.

Dennery village sits on a hillside overlooking the Atlantic Ocean. During the day, it's quiet and full of charm. You can walk along the coast, talk to local fishermen, or explore the nearby Dennery waterfall. The people here are friendly and proud of their heritage. They are happy to share their way of life with curious visitors.

But the real magic happens on **Sunday night**, when Dennery hosts its famous **Fish Fiesta**—a fun-filled street party right by the waterfront. Locals cook fresh fish, lobster, and conch in so many delicious ways—fried, grilled, stewed. The music starts early and lasts late into the night. You'll hear soca, reggae, and local Dennery Segment music, with everyone dancing and enjoying the good vibes.

Unlike the more touristy events on the west coast, the Dennery Fish Fiesta feels truly local. It's a place where you can connect with real people, taste homemade food, and be part of something alive and joyful. If you enjoy live music and street food, this is an event you must not miss.

There are also nearby attractions worth exploring before the party starts—like the Mandele Point viewpoint or Fond d'Or Nature Reserve, where you can learn about the island's colonial past and wildlife.

Whether you're coming for the food, the music, or the community spirit, Dennery will leave you with warm memories. It's not just a place to visit—it's a place to feel alive.

Chapter 7: Southern Gems & Rural Villages

Laborie's Hidden Coastal Charms

Laborie is one of St. Lucia's best-kept secrets. Tucked away on the island's southern coast, this quiet fishing village feels like stepping back in time. There are no big hotels, no crowds, and no noise—just peace, friendly people, and natural beauty everywhere you look.

When you arrive in Laborie, you'll notice how calm and welcoming the town feels. The streets are lined with colorful wooden houses, and locals often greet you with a smile or wave. Many visitors say it feels more like staying with a big family than being a tourist.

The beach in Laborie is one of its biggest treasures. It's long, clean, and never too busy.

You can walk along the soft sand, swim in the clear blue water, or just sit under a palm tree and listen to the waves. If you're lucky, you might see fishermen bringing in their daily catch. It's a great way to connect with local life.

Food here is simple but tasty. You can try grilled fish, fried plantains, and homemade bread at small family-run restaurants or snack shops. One of the best things to do is buy fresh fruits from the roadside stands—mangoes, bananas, and coconuts are everywhere.

Laborie also loves music. If you visit during a weekend or local event, you might hear live drumming or see people dancing in the streets. There's a strong community spirit here, and visitors are always welcome to join in.

This village is perfect for travelers who want to slow down and enjoy the little things. It's not about fancy attractions—it's about feeling at home, breathing fresh air, and experiencing the real St. Lucia.

If you want to explore deeper, there are nearby nature trails and local farms that offer tours. But even just walking through Laborie, talking to locals, or watching the sunset over the sea will give you lasting memories.

So, if you're looking for a peaceful, authentic part of St. Lucia, make sure to stop in Laborie. It may be quiet, but it will speak to your heart

Choiseul Arts & Craft Village

Choiseul is a special place in St. Lucia where tradition and creativity live side by side. This quiet village is known all over the island for its amazing handmade crafts, friendly people, and peaceful vibe. If you enjoy local art and culture, Choiseul should be high on your list.

As soon as you arrive, you'll notice the beauty of the hills, trees, and the calm pace of life. What makes Choiseul really stand out is its strong connection to the island's heritage. Many of the villagers here are skilled artists and crafters, keeping old traditions alive through their work.

You'll find hand-woven baskets, pottery, wood carvings, and colorful fabrics—all made by local hands. One of the best places to visit is the **Choiseul Arts and Crafts Centre**, where you can watch artisans at work and buy their creations directly. Every item tells a story, and many are made from natural materials like banana leaves, coconut shells, and clay from the island.

Talking to the crafters is part of the fun. They're proud of what they do and happy to explain how their pieces are made. It's more than just shopping—it's a learning experience and a chance to support local talent.

The village is also close to nature. You can take a short hike to waterfalls or visit farms growing fruits, spices, and herbs. Many locals will even invite you to try fresh fruits straight from the tree. The area feels untouched by time, offering a glimpse into how St. Lucia looked before modern resorts arrived.

There are a few small eateries in Choiseul, often run by families, where you can enjoy creole dishes like fish stew, green figs, and rice and beans. It's simple, fresh, and full of flavor.

Choiseul is not flashy or touristy, but that's what makes it special. It's a perfect place to slow down, learn something new, and meet people who live with heart and soul. Whether you leave with a carved mask or just good memories, this village will stay with you.

Vieux Fort & Sandy Beach Exploration

Vieux Fort is the southernmost town in St. Lucia, and it's full of surprises. It's not as busy as Castries or as famous as Soufrière, but it has its own charm—and a beach that's hard to beat. If you like wide open spaces, ocean views, and a mix of local life and hidden gems, this is a great place to explore.

One of the top attractions in Vieux Fort is **Sandy Beach**. The name says it all—it's long, sandy, and open. You can walk for a mile and barely see anyone else. The waves here are gentle in some parts and stronger in others, making it great for both relaxing and kite-surfing. In fact, Sandy Beach is one of the best places on the island for wind sports, and you might see locals and visitors flying across the water with colorful kites.

But even if you're not into sports, the beach is perfect for a quiet day under the sun. There are shaded areas, food vendors selling grilled seafood, and a few beach bars where you can grab a cold drink and watch the waves roll in. The sunsets here are especially beautiful—fiery orange skies over the calm sea.

In town, Vieux Fort offers a glimpse of everyday island life. There’s a large open-air market where you can buy fresh produce, spices, and snacks. It’s busy, colorful, and full of friendly faces. You’ll hear music, smell local cooking, and see how people live day by day.

The town also has some history. You can visit the **Moule à Chique Lighthouse**, which sits on a hill with one of the best views in St. Lucia. From the top, you can see both the Atlantic

Ocean and the Caribbean Sea. It's a quiet spot with a big reward.

Vieux Fort is also close to the island's international airport, so it's a good place to start or end your journey. It may not be as well-known, but that's what makes it feel real and refreshing.

If you want to experience a different side of St. Lucia—less polished but full of soul—don't miss Vieux Fort and its beautiful Sandy Beach. It's a part of the island that leaves you feeling free and fully alive.

Chapter 8: Adventure & Outdoor Activities

Zip-lining & Rainforest Canopy Tours

If you're looking for a fun way to see St. Lucia's beautiful rainforests, zip-lining is a must-try. It's exciting, safe, and gives you a bird's-eye view of the island's lush green jungle. You'll feel the rush of wind as you glide between giant trees, flying high above rivers, valleys, and tropical plants.

There are several great places for zip-lining in St. Lucia. One of the most popular is **Treetop Adventure Park** in Dennery. It has 12 zip lines, including one of the longest and fastest lines on the island. The guides are friendly and well-trained, and they'll help you every step of the way—even if it's your first time. You'll also get a short safety lesson before starting, so you can enjoy the ride with peace of mind.

Another great place is the **Rainforest Adventures** near Babonneau. This one includes not just zip-lining, but also a scenic aerial tram ride and nature walks. The tram takes you slowly through the forest canopy, where you can spot birds, lizards, and colorful flowers. It's perfect if you want both a thrill and a chance to relax and enjoy nature.

Most zip-line tours take about 2–3 hours and are suitable for kids (usually 8 and older) and adults. Wear comfortable clothes, closed shoes, and don't forget to bring a camera or GoPro—some lines offer amazing photo opportunities!

Zip-lining in St. Lucia is more than just a ride. It's a chance to connect with nature, feel the island's wild side, and enjoy something unforgettable. Whether you're visiting as a couple, with family, or solo, this activity is sure to be a highlight of your trip. Don't be surprised if you leave the forest with a huge smile and a desire to do it all over again.

Scuba Diving, Snorkeling & Marine Parks

St. Lucia is just as stunning below the water as it is above. Whether you're an experienced diver or a first-time snorkeler, the island's warm, clear waters are full of colorful marine life, coral reefs, and even shipwrecks. It's a paradise for ocean lovers.

One of the best areas for underwater adventures is the **Soufrière Marine Management Area** (SMMA), located on the west coast of the island. This protected zone includes famous spots like **Anse Chastanet**, **Superman's Flight**, and **Piton Wall**. These sites are great for both diving and snorkeling, offering vibrant coral gardens, tropical fish, and even sea turtles.

For snorkeling, **Anse Cochon** and **Sugar Beach** are two of the top beaches. You can walk right into the water and start exploring just a few feet from shore. The visibility is usually excellent, and the calm waters make it easy to float and enjoy the sights below.

If you're new to scuba diving, many dive shops offer beginner courses and one-day discovery dives. You'll learn the basics, practice in shallow water, and then go out with an instructor to a real dive site. For certified divers, there are plenty of guided dives, night dives, and even wreck dives available.

Popular dive operators include **Scuba St. Lucia**, **Action Adventure Divers**, and **Dive Fair Helen**. They provide all the gear, and most will even pick you up from your hotel. Safety is a top priority, and the instructors are professional and knowledgeable.

Don't forget to bring a waterproof camera if you have one. The colors underwater are stunning—bright parrotfish, sea fans swaying with the current, and coral heads teeming with life.

Scuba diving and snorkeling in St. Lucia is more than just an activity—it's an experience of peace, wonder, and adventure. Floating through the warm Caribbean Sea, surrounded by marine life, is something you won't forget. It's perfect for couples, solo travelers, and families who want to make amazing memories together.

River Tubing & Waterfall Safaris

If you love the water but want something different from the beach, river tubing and waterfall safaris are great ways to enjoy St. Lucia's natural side. These adventures take you deep into the heart of the island, where you can float, splash, and soak in the beauty of the rainforest.

River tubing is a relaxing and fun activity that involves riding down a gentle river in a big inflatable tube. One of the best places to do this is the **La Sorcière River** near Dennery. The current is calm, so it's safe even for beginners and kids. Along the way, you'll glide under shady trees, pass rock formations, and maybe even spot birds or little crabs on the riverbanks.

Guides float with you and make sure everyone is safe and having fun. They also tell stories about the area and point out interesting plants or animals. It's a peaceful experience with just enough excitement to keep things interesting. You don't need to swim, but you should be comfortable in water.

Waterfall safaris, on the other hand, take you through trails and forests to some of the island's most beautiful hidden waterfalls. One popular spot is **Toraille Waterfall**, where you can stand under the rushing water for a refreshing natural shower. Another favorite is **Enbas Saut**, a more off-the-beaten-path trail in the Edmund Forest Reserve that leads to twin waterfalls surrounded by tall trees and birdsong.

Many tours combine hiking, swimming, and even a picnic lunch by the water. It's the perfect mix of adventure and relaxation. Be sure to wear comfortable shoes, bring a towel, and pack a change of clothes—you *will* get wet!

These activities are ideal for anyone who wants to escape the crowds and enjoy the peaceful side of St. Lucia. Whether you're floating on a river or standing under a waterfall, you'll feel a deep connection to nature. It's calming, refreshing, and something you'll carry in your heart long after you've returned home.

Chapter 9: Eat, Drink & Stay

Classic Street Food & Local Restaurants

One of the best ways to experience the real St. Lucia is through its food. The island is full of flavors that reflect its culture, history, and love for good cooking. From tasty street snacks to family-run restaurants, you'll find something for every kind of traveler.

If you're walking around towns like Castries, Soufrière, or Gros Islet, you'll see small food stalls called "cook shops" or "roadside vendors." Don't pass them by! These little spots serve up hot, homemade meals that are both affordable and full of flavor. Try a **roti**—a soft wrap filled with curried chicken, beef, or vegetables. It's a local favorite and perfect for eating on the go.

Green fig and saltfish is St. Lucia's national dish, and you'll find it at many spots, especially during breakfast. It's made with boiled green bananas and salted codfish, mixed with onions, peppers, and spices. It might sound unusual, but it's delicious and full of island flavor.

If you're craving something grilled, visit the **Gros Islet Friday Night Street Party**, where the streets come alive with the smell of barbecue. Fresh fish, lobster, and chicken are grilled right in front of you. Pair it with a local Piton beer or some homemade rum punch, and you're set.

Local restaurants also offer great dining experiences. Try **The Pink Plantation House** near Castries for a lovely view and tasty Creole dishes made with local ingredients. **Orlando's**

in Soufrière is another popular spot where the chef mixes traditional island recipes with modern touches.

Many places use fresh, local ingredients, and St. Lucians take pride in their cooking. Whether you're sitting in a fancy seaside restaurant or eating jerk chicken from a roadside grill, the food here has heart and soul.

So come hungry! Food in St. Lucia isn't just about eating—it's about enjoying, sharing, and discovering the island's warm, flavorful spirit.

Boutique Hotels, B&Bs & Eco-Lodges

St. Lucia has places to stay for every kind of traveler, but if you want something more personal, warm, and unique, consider staying at a boutique hotel, B&B, or eco-lodge. These places give you a real taste of island life, with friendly hosts, beautiful surroundings, and lots of charm.

In the town of Soufrière, there are several small hotels and guesthouses with amazing views of the Pitons. One favorite is **La Haut Plantation**, which sits high on a hill and offers cozy rooms with balconies looking over the sea and mountains. It's peaceful, full of local character, and close to many top attractions.

If you love nature, try staying at an **eco-lodge** like **Fond Doux Eco Resort**. It's a working cocoa plantation with cute cottages surrounded by lush greenery. You'll hear birds in the morning and fall asleep to the sounds of the forest at night. It's a great choice for travelers who want comfort while staying close to nature.

B&Bs (bed and breakfasts) are another good option, especially for couples or solo travelers who want a homey place to stay. Many are run by locals who will treat you like family. They'll even help you plan your trip, suggest hidden spots to visit, and cook delicious island breakfasts.

If you're staying near the north of the island, places like **Villa Beach Cottages** or **Bel Jou Hotel** in Castries are peaceful and welcoming. They give you easy access to beaches, shopping, and restaurants, while still feeling quiet and personal.

These smaller stays are often more affordable than big resorts, and you get a closer connection to the local culture. You can sit on the porch, talk with your hosts, and really feel like you're part of the community.

No matter where you choose, St. Lucia's boutique hotels and eco-lodges offer more than just a room—they offer real memories. You'll leave with stories, new friendships, and a strong desire to return.

Wellness Retreats & Spa Experiences

St. Lucia isn't just a place to explore—it's also a perfect place to relax, heal, and take care of your body and mind. The island is known for its peaceful nature, fresh air, and warm energy, making it ideal for wellness and spa getaways.

If you're looking to unwind, you'll find many **wellness resorts** that offer yoga, meditation, massages, and more. One of the most popular is **The BodyHoliday** in Cap Estate. This all-inclusive resort focuses on wellness, with daily spa treatments, fitness classes, and healthy meals. You can try tai chi by the ocean, or get a relaxing massage in a treehouse-style room surrounded by nature.

Another great place is **Soufrière's Sugar Beach, A Viceroy Resort**, where the spa is hidden in the rainforest. It's like stepping into a peaceful world of calm. You can enjoy mud wraps, facials, and hot stone massages, all while listening to the sounds of the forest and nearby waterfalls.

For a more natural experience, visit the **Sulphur Springs**—the Caribbean's only drive-in volcano. Here, you can soak in warm, mineral-rich waters and cover yourself in volcanic mud. It's fun, healthy, and leaves your skin feeling smooth and refreshed. Many locals believe the mud has healing powers.

Several smaller wellness spots also offer yoga retreats, juice cleanses, and private coaching. These are perfect if you're on a journey to reset your mind and body. Some even offer beachside classes at sunrise, helping you feel balanced and connected to nature.

You don't need to be on a retreat to enjoy wellness in St. Lucia. Many hotels and eco-lodges offer simple spa services or in-room massages. Even taking a long walk along the beach, swimming in clear water, or sipping fresh coconut water can feel like a healing experience.

In St. Lucia, wellness is a way of life. You'll find yourself breathing deeper, sleeping better, and smiling more. Whether you come to relax for a few days or spend a week in full retreat mode, you'll leave the island feeling lighter, calmer, and more alive than ever

Chapter 10: Traveler Tips & Resources

Health, Safety & Travel Insurance

Your health and safety are very important when traveling, and St. Lucia is generally a safe and friendly island. Most visitors have a smooth and enjoyable stay, but it's always wise to be prepared.

Let's start with **health**. You don't need any special vaccinations to enter St. Lucia in 2025, but it's a good idea to be up to date with your routine vaccines like tetanus, measles, and hepatitis A. The tap water in most hotels is safe to drink, but if you have a sensitive stomach, bottled water is easy to find. Tropical weather can be hot and humid, so be sure to drink plenty of fluids and wear sunscreen every day.

There are pharmacies across the island in major towns like Castries, Soufrière, and Rodney Bay. Most over-the-counter medicine is available, but if you take prescription medication, bring enough with you to last the whole trip.

Now, on to **safety**. St. Lucia is peaceful and locals are very welcoming. Still, just like anywhere in the world, you should use common sense. Don't leave your phone or bag unattended, especially on the beach. Avoid walking alone in unfamiliar areas late at night, and always lock your hotel or rental doors. Use only official taxis or hotel-approved drivers for transport.

Finally, **travel insurance** is something many travelers forget, but it's very important. It can cover things like lost baggage, flight delays, or unexpected illness. Some insurance also includes adventure coverage, which is helpful if you're planning to hike the Pitons or go diving.

In 2025, some travel insurance plans even offer COVID-19-related coverage, so it's worth checking before you buy.

In case of emergency, dial **999** or **911** to reach the police or ambulance services. Hospitals and clinics are available in both the north and south parts of the island, with the main public hospital being in Castries.

In short, St. Lucia is a safe and healthy place to visit, but taking a few precautions and having insurance will help you enjoy your trip with peace of mind.

Transport, Ferry & Car Rental Guide

Getting around St. Lucia can be part of the adventure! The island isn't huge, but there's still plenty to explore, from hidden beaches to mountain villages. Here's a guide to help you choose the best way to travel around in 2025.

Taxis are common and easy to find at the airport, hotels, and popular tourist spots. Most taxis in St. Lucia do not have meters, so always agree on the fare before you start your journey. Rates are often fixed for popular routes (like airport to hotel), and drivers are usually friendly and knowledgeable.

If you want to explore at your own pace, **car rentals** are a great option. You'll find rental companies at the airports and in towns like Rodney Bay and Soufrière. You'll need a valid driver's license from your home country and a temporary St. Lucian permit, which costs about $20 USD. Keep in mind that St. Lucians drive on the **left side** of the road. Some roads are narrow, winding, and bumpy—especially in the countryside—so drive carefully and take your time.

Ferries are also available if you want to travel to nearby islands. From St. Lucia, you can take a ferry to **Martinique**, **Dominica**, or **Guadeloupe**. The journey is scenic, and it's a fun way to experience more of the Caribbean. You'll need your passport and may need to go through immigration, so plan ahead.

Minibuses (public transportation) are a budget-friendly way to get around. They run between towns and are used mainly by locals. Look for the green license plates that begin with an "M." They don't have fixed schedules, and drivers usually wait until the bus is full before leaving. It's cheap and a real local experience, but it might not be comfortable for long rides or with luggage.

For short distances, walking is safe in most areas, especially in tourist zones like Rodney Bay. Many hotels also offer **shuttle services** to nearby beaches or attractions.

If you're staying in a resort, ask the front desk for transportation help. Whether you rent a car, take a ferry, or hop in a taxi, getting around St. Lucia is part of the fun!

Apps, Websites & Booking Resources

In 2025, planning and enjoying your trip to St. Lucia is easier than ever, thanks to helpful apps and websites. Whether you're booking a room, finding places to eat, or getting directions to the Pitons, these tools can save you time and make your trip smooth and enjoyable.

Let's start with **booking your trip**. Use websites like **Booking.com**, **Expedia**, or **Airbnb** to find hotels, guesthouses, or vacation rentals across the island. If you're looking for eco-lodges or small local stays, also try **Agoda** or **VRBO**. Many travelers use **TripAdvisor** to read reviews before booking a place or tour.

For **flights**, apps like **Skyscanner**, **Google Flights**, or **Hopper** are great for comparing prices and setting alerts when fares drop. If you're flying in from another Caribbean island, check local airlines like **Caribbean Airlines** or **LIAT**.

Once you're on the island, apps like **Google Maps** or **Maps.me** are helpful for finding your way around. Some areas have spotty signals, especially in rural or mountain regions, so download maps offline in advance. If you're hiking the Pitons or going deep into the forest, consider a hiking app like **AllTrails**.

Need a ride? While **Uber and Lyft** aren't available in St. Lucia, many hotels and tours use **WhatsApp** to communicate with guests. It's very popular on the island, so download it before you go—it's useful for contacting drivers, guides, or local services.

For restaurants and attractions, apps like **TripAdvisor**, **Google Reviews**, or even **Instagram** can help you discover hidden gems. Many local restaurants now post their menus or food specials online, so checking their social media pages is a good idea.

Conclusion

As your journey through the pages of this guide comes to an end, a new one is just beginning—**your own adventure in St. Lucia**.

This island is not just a place you visit. It's a feeling you carry with you long after the trip is over. It's the sound of waves hitting the shore, the scent of spices in the market, the rhythm of drums at a street party, and the quiet magic of a sunset behind the Pitons. It's the laughter you share with strangers who feel like friends, the stories you'll tell long after you've returned home, and the peace you find in nature's embrace.

Traveling to St. Lucia is more than ticking off tourist spots. It's about being present. It's about waking up with the sun, tasting something new, dancing without fear, and letting the island show you who you really are when you slow down and just live.

Whether you spend your time climbing mountains, relaxing on a quiet beach, sailing into the blue Caribbean Sea, or learning about the culture and people—you are creating memories that will stay with you for a lifetime.

Don’t worry about doing everything. Just do what feels right for you. Some of the best moments in St. Lucia happen when you put away the map, talk to locals, try that strange dish, or take that unexpected turn down a quiet road. That’s where the real magic lives—in the simple, surprising moments.

As you plan your trip or reflect on your time here, remember this: **St. Lucia has a way of changing people.** You come for the beauty, but you leave with something deeper—a sense of calm, a heart full of gratitude, and a new perspective on life.

So pack light, bring an open heart, and come ready to feel alive. Let the island welcome you, teach you, surprise you, and, most of all, inspire you.

St. Lucia is waiting for you.

And trust me—**you'll never be the same.**

Printed in Dunstable, United Kingdom

63837313R00050